TALKING ABOUT

Islamophobia

WHAT IS IT AND HOW DO WE CHALLENGE IT? A BEGINNER'S GUIDE FOR CHILDREN

Sabeena Akhtar & Naïma B. Robert

First published in paperback in Great Britain in 2022 by Wayland

Editorial: Nicola Edwards and Sarah Ridley
Design: Rocket Design (East Anglia) Ltd and Lisa Peacock
Artwork by Oli Frape

ISBN 978 1 5263 1338 6 (paperback)
10 9 8 7 6 5 4 3 2 1

MIX
Paper from responsible sources
FSC® C104740
www.fsc.org

Wayland, an imprint of
Hachette Children's Group
Part of Hodder and Stoughton
Carmelite House
50 Victoria Embankment
London EC4Y 0DZ

An Hachette UK Company
www.hachette.co.uk
www.hachettechildrens.co.uk

Printed and bound in Dubai

The authors would like to give their sincere thanks to all who contributed to this book, with special thanks to Dr Sofia Rehman and Dr Mustapha Sheikh.

The Publisher would like to thank Zakirah Alam and Clive Lawton.

Picture acknowledgements:

Getty Images: Leemage/Corbis 14; New York Daily News 7; Guillaume Pinon/NurPhoto Getty Images 25; Jack Taylor 12; Stanislav Krasilnikov 16
Shutterstock: Andrey Burstein 20; Dev Chatterjee 23; Darrenp 4; Eddie Hernandez Photos 19b; Julien_j 10; Littlenystock 16; Monkey Business Images 17; Alessia Pierdomenico 29; Sandra Sanders 19t; Polina Valetenkova 6.
Wikimedia: Engraving Antwerp 1631/PD/St Edmund Campion SJ 8br; John Foxes Book of Martyrs, 1563/PD 8bl.

CONTENTS

WHY DO WE NEED TO TALK ABOUT **ISLAMOPHOBIA?**

On 15 March 2019, a man walked into a mosque in Christchurch, New Zealand, during the Friday prayers. There were hundreds of people inside the mosque. He was greeted with "Hello, brother" as he entered, and that was when he started shooting.

He spent six minutes inside the mosque, shooting indiscriminately, killing 42 people. Then he drove to the Linwood Islamic Centre and began shooting again. This time, seven people died.

The attacker had livestreamed 17 minutes of the carnage to 200 viewers on Facebook and, within 24 hours, there were 1.5 million videos of it in circulation. The gunman even left a manifesto to try and justify his crimes.

This cowardly attack brought home to millions the horrifying reality of Islamophobia.

Following the attack, many people expressed their horror at what had taken place and mourned the loss of the 49 people who had died.

This shocking act motivated us to write this book. For many onlookers, it would be easy to think of Islamophobia as a series of terrible isolated incidents such as this, but such acts do not occur out of nowhere. They are the result of a 'culture' of Islamophobia that exists in society and normalises the hatred and dehumanisation of Muslims. In his manifesto, the New Zealand gunman quoted and referred to many mainstream news articles as a justification for his awful actions. Although he acted alone, he had been influenced by Islamophobia in wider society. It is our hope that we can tackle and resist Islamophobia, so that we can all live in a more tolerant and peaceful society. In order to do this, it is important to be able to recognise the many ways in which Islamophobia exists.

What do we mean by a culture of Islamophobia?

Islamophobia is everywhere in society. We particularly see it in media creations of harmful stereotypes about Muslims which reinforce the idea that they are scary or dangerous. As a result of this, people begin to treat Muslims (and people they assume to be Muslim) with suspicion and fear. Representations of Muslims on TV and in films also embed this idea. Most Muslim characters we see on our screens are criminals or dangerous. Some politicians also use this fear to pass laws and say things that are harmful to Muslims and perpetuate the idea that Muslims cannot be trusted in society or are dangerous to it. The result of all this is a culture where is it okay to treat Muslims unfairly or with suspicion. We'll talk about this in more detail later in the book.

A better future

As authors and mothers, we can't help but think about all the children growing up in a confusing world of multiculturalism and tolerance on the one hand, and hatred and suspicion on the other. And it was the thought of these children that made us talk about what we could do – and how we could help.

In this book, we hope to bring issues out into the open so that they may be discussed and understood. Throughout the book we'll ask you to think about different aspects of Islamophobia for yourself and come up with ideas about how to deal with them.

Worth fighting for

Working on this book wasn't easy or pleasant. We want to hold on to the hope of an open, tolerant society, where all can live according to their conscience and co-create a safe space for all – but we cannot deny the facts. The political, social and cultural evidence points to an increase in discrimination and prejudice in our society. It becomes a duty for us all to call it out and resist, in the name of all that is good and worth fighting for.

Because the thing about human history is this: it keeps repeating itself, again and again and again, until we learn the lessons and do things differently. Education can do that. It is our aim that this book will allow us to show Islamophobia for what it is: just another link in the chain of discrimination, prejudice and fear that has always been a threat to justice and peace for all people, everywhere.

WHAT IS ISLAM?

Islam is the name of the religion practised by Muslims, who believe in one God, Allah. Muslims worship Allah through the teachings set out in the Qur'an by the Prophet Muhammad (peace be upon him), to whom the Qur'an was revealed.

Muslims believe that the Qur'an is the direct word of God and try to live their lives in accordance with its teachings. The holy book contains a comprehensive belief system often described as a 'way of life' rather than just a religion.

Underpinning all Muslims' lives are the five pillars of Islam:

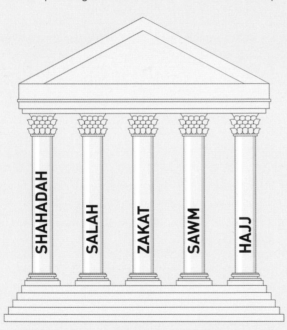

SHAHADAH   SALAH   ZAKAT   SAWM   HAJJ

Shahadah – the Muslim declaration of faith: "There is no God but Allah, and Muhammad (pbuh) is His messenger"

Salah (prayer) – the act of praying five times a day

Zakat – giving away money, usually to charity

Sawm – fasting during the month of Ramadan

Hajj – the pilgrimage to Mecca in Saudi Arabia that all Muslims hope to make at least once in their lifetime.

Justice, equality and fairness

The five pillars are the main teachings of Islam but, historically and spiritually, Islam means much more than this to Muslims. Revealed to the Prophet Muhammad (pbuh) 1,400 years ago, Islam came as a religion of social justice. Muslims throughout history have been taught to stand up for justice, equality and fairness. This ranges from being kind and respectful to family and neighbours, to challenging injustices in society.

> *"… Be just, for it is closest to God-consciousness …" (Qur'an 5:8)*

Muslim activists for social justice

Political activist Malcolm X and superstar boxer Muhammad Ali campaigned for civil rights for African Americans. As black men, these pioneering activists experienced racism and discrimination throughout their lives, but were also treated with suspicion because they were Muslim. Muhammad Ali risked his boxing career and Malcolm X was eventually assassinated because of their belief in justice and equality for the black community.

In 1967, Muhammad Ali refused to fight in the Vietnam War:

"I will not disgrace my religion, my people, or myself by becoming a tool to enslave those who are fighting for their own justice, freedom, and equality."

World heavyweight boxing champion Muhammad Ali (left) with his friend and mentor, Malcolm X, in New York, USA, in 1964.

Where do Muslims live?

Since Islam is the second largest religion in the world after Christianity, and numbers over 1.9 billion followers, Muslims live across the globe in varying percentages of the population. For instance, in Indonesia, Muslims make up 87 per cent of the population. In Nigeria 50 per cent of the population is Muslim, while in New Zealand it is just 1 per cent. In the UK, Muslims account for about 5 per cent of the population.

Muslims have rich and unique cultures, hailing from all over the world, including Tanzania, India, Pakistan, Senegal, Somalia, Malaysia, Albania, Turkey, Lebanon and many more places. Although the locations, languages and cultural practices of Muslims across the world may vary, they are all unified in their belief in God.

WHAT IS RELIGIOUS INTOLERANCE AND DISCRIMINATION?

Religious intolerance is an unwillingness to let people of all faiths follow the beliefs and practices of their religion. Religious discrimination is treating people differently or taking away their rights because of their religious beliefs.

What does religious intolerance look like?

Religious intolerance can operate on several levels in society. At the highest level, it can mean that there are laws in place that discriminate against members of religions other than the state religion. These laws could make it illegal for followers to attend a place of worship or practice their religion.

But religious intolerance doesn't have to be enshrined in law to cause a problem. It can also happen when members of a society stereotype followers of a minority religion, place them under suspicion or make them feel unwelcome. In Tudor England, changes in the state religion led to persecution on a large scale in the sixteenth century (see below).

Mary I (ruled 1553–1558) was a devout Roman Catholic who wanted to reverse the Protestantism of her brother Edward VI's reign. More than 280 Protestant dissenters were burnt at the stake during her reign, including Bishop Latimer and Bishop Ridley, shown in this engraving.

During Elizabeth I's reign (1558–1603), anyone caught saying the Latin mass or leading Catholic services was considered a traitor. Scores of priests, such as St Edmund Campion, shown here, were put to death for treason.

History is full of examples of individuals and groups being persecuted due to their religious beliefs. Here are two further examples.

The Reconquista and the Spanish Inquisition

The Reconquista, or Reconquest of Spain, took place between the eighth and fifteenth centuries. Christian states in medieval Spain and Portugal fought to gain control of the Iberian Peninsula, lands which had been occupied since the eighth century by the Moors, who were Muslims.

The Spanish Inquisition was set up in 1478 by Queen Isabella and King Ferdinand of Spain, with the blessing of Pope Sixtus IV. The king and queen wanted to create a purely Catholic country, united in belief and loyal only to them and the Catholic Church. Courts controlled by the chief inquisitor listened to the pleas of civilians who claimed to have converted to Christianity to see if they still held Jewish or Muslim beliefs. Torture was often used and many were burnt at the stake.

After their victory against the Moors in the Reconquista, Ferdinand and Isabella stepped up the pressure on Jewish people in Spain, many of whom had lived in Spain for centuries at this point. In 1492, a decree of expulsion required Jews to leave the country or to give up their religion and convert to Christianity. Then, in 1499, the same was required of the Muslim Moors. After some resistance, the Moors were chased out of Spain.

Hitler's Germany before and during the Second World War

Fast forward to the twentieth century. Germany's defeat in the First World War and the accompanying economic hardship paved the way for the spread of anti-semitic ideas. The growing intolerance of Jews was not founded on religious principles as such (they were not regarded as 'heretics') but on the ideas of German nationalism. Jewish people were increasingly portrayed as outsiders, inferior to true (Aryan) Germans. During the first six years of Hitler's dictatorship, from 1933 until the outbreak of war in 1939, Jews felt the effects of more than 400 decrees and regulations that restricted all aspects of their public and private lives. Worse was to come as the Nazi party put into action its plan to exterminate all Jews.

These are some of the laws that were implemented to control, and eventually exterminate, the Jews. About six million Jews were murdered during the Holocaust.

Jewish people were:

- stripped of German citizenship
- not allowed to hold public office
- not allowed to intermarry
- not allowed to practise as doctors and lawyers
- not allowed to own their own business
- not allowed to attend state schools
- denied treatment at state hospitals
- made to identify as Jews on passports and identity documents
- excluded from parks, theatres and cinemas.

Religious discrimination today

In light of the violence and bloodshed that has resulted from religious intolerance and persecution throughout history, there are now laws to prevent religious discrimination. They are enshrined in national and international law systems.

For instance, in many countries around the world, including the UK, several laws protect the religious beliefs and practices of religious minorities. Here are extracts from two such laws, the Human Rights Act and the Equality Act 2010 (UK).

Article 9 of the Human Rights Act
Freedom of thought, conscience and religion

1 Everyone has the right to freedom of thought, conscience and religion; this right includes freedom to change his religion or belief and freedom, either alone or in community with others and in public or private, to manifest his religion or belief, in worship, teaching, practice and observance.

2 Freedom to manifest one's religion or beliefs shall be subject only to such limitations as are prescribed by law and are necessary in a democratic society in the interests of public safety, for the protection of public order, health or morals, or for the protection of the rights and freedoms of others.

Article 9 protects:

- the freedom to change religion or belief

- the freedom to exercise religion or belief publicly or privately, alone or with others

- the freedom to exercise religion or belief in worship, teaching, practice and observance, and

- the right to have no religion (to be atheist or agnostic) or to have non-religious beliefs protected (such as a belief in the need for urgent action to tackle climate change or philosophical beliefs, such as pacifism or veganism).

People gather in Paris to protest against climate change.

Equality Act 2010

The Equality Act 2010 is a way to protect the rights of all individuals and ensure equality of opportunity for all. According to this act, no individual may be discriminated against, or treated unfairly, due to certain special characteristics, including religion or belief. According to the act:

1 Religion means any religion, and a reference to religion includes a reference to a lack of religion.

2 Belief means any religious or philosophical belief, and a reference to belief includes a reference to a lack of belief.

3 In relation to the protected characteristic of religion or belief:

a A reference to a person who has a particular protected characteristic is a reference to a person of a particular religion or belief;

b A reference to persons who share a protected characteristic is a reference to persons who are of the same religion or belief.

Persistent intolerance

So you can see that, by and large, religious intolerance and discrimination are illegal in the UK and similar laws exist in other countries. In some countries though, such as Switzerland, Muslims have seen articles of their faith, such as the wearing of a burka or a niqab in public, legislated against. In New Zealand, the freedom to act in accordance with religious belief is not as wide as the freedom to hold those beliefs: "Limitations can be imposed on how religion and belief is expressed, particularly where matters of public safety or the fundamental rights and freedoms of others are affected."

So why does intolerance persist? And what does it look like in modern society? And why does discrimination, in particular Islamophobia, exist, in spite of the legislation that is in place to protect people of faith? These are some of the questions we are going to explore in the coming pages.

TALKING POINTS

Play a game with your classmates: you have three seconds to say the first words that pop into your head when you think of the words Muslim or Islam.

Discuss your answers and what may have influenced your responses.

WHAT IS ISLAMOPHOBIA?

Islamophobia is fear of and discrimination against Muslims – in short, anti-Muslim racism. Unfortunately, there are many people who refuse to acknowledge that Islamophobia exists or that it is a structural problem, meaning it is embedded in society through government policies, laws and the media (see pages 20-21 and 24-27 for more on this). There are others who have used far-right populism and anti-Muslim sentiment to achieve political gain or further their careers.

Politics and Islamophobia

Take the 2016 EU Referendum held in the UK, when citizens of the UK were asked in an advisory referendum to vote to stay, or leave, the European Union (EU). One poster commissioned by the UK Independence Party (UKIP) showed a column of Syrian refugees next to the words 'Breaking point' to illustrate the idea of the UK being swamped by 'foreigners' because of its membership of the EU. In fact, most of the Syrians escaping war at that time still live in refugee camps in Turkey, Jordan and Lebanon, while a proportion have settled in Germany and a few other European countries, including the UK. The purpose of such imagery and language is to falsely infer that Muslims pose a threat and want to take over.

Nigel Farage, then leader of the UK Independence Party, presents the 'Breaking Point' poster at a press conference during the 2016 EU Referendum.

Politicians should choose their words carefully but, sadly, as happened during the UK EU Referendum and elsewhere around the world, some politicians have attacked certain groups in order to win popularity and even elections. Instead of challenging racism in all its forms, they have allowed divisive views to take root in society.

Defining Islamophobia

There isn't one definition of Islamophobia but individuals, politicians, academics and international organisations continue to work towards an accepted definition. Dr Mustapha Sheikh is an academic who addresses the challenge of Islamophobia. He has co-authored the fatwa on the necessity of opposing Islamophobia, which has been read by people around the world. Here's what he has to say on the subject:

"We must aspire to an understanding of Islamophobia – an understanding that will both illuminate the complex nature of the system of Islamophobia and enable resistance to it. Muslims globally are affected by Islamophobia in ways that they know and understand and in ways that they don't so easily perceive or understand. What each and every Muslim can relate to, however, is the hurt, anxiety, anger, pain, confusion, exclusion, stigmatisation, abuse, exploitation and erasure that arises in connection with their Muslimness.

"Nothing is more important to me than the work I am doing responding to the challenge of Islamophobia. A key facet of this work is to support the new definition of Islamophobia: 'Islamophobia is a form of racism that targets expressions of Muslimness or perceived Muslimness', *for no form of resistance is possible if we are unable to identify what we are up against."*

Islam and racism

It is important to understand that Islamophobia is a type of racism. Even though Islam is one of the most diverse religions, Islamophobia represents Muslims as a group of people with shared characteristics, in the same way that 'races' were represented in the past. These racist stereotypes can lead to discrimination in all areas of life. At the root of Islamophobia is the idea that Muslims are a dangerous 'other', wanting to take over or harm people through terrorism (see page 15). When an entire religion or people are racialised and viewed with hostility it becomes easier for people to justify discrimination against them.

TALKING POINTS

Imagine you go into a shop in your school uniform and the shopkeeper refuses to allow you in because another pupil at your school was found shoplifting. They tell you they know what all the pupils at the school are like and that they don't trust any of you because of the actions of that pupil. How would this make you feel – and why?

WHERE DOES ISLAMOPHOBIA COME FROM?

The word 'Islamophobia' is a relatively new one, but throughout history, many cultures have fostered a fear of the 'other' or people who they deemed to be different to them.

The Crusades

The Crusades were a series of wars lasting about 200 years. They started in 1095 when Pope Urban II promised forgiveness from sins if knights went on a crusade to 'liberate' the Holy Land from Arab Muslims. Religious authorities and various European powers supported the many bloody battles that ensued, both for religious and political reasons.

The Crusades are often seen as a potent symbol of a historical animosity between Christians and Muslims, an animosity that is often framed as a 'clash of civilisations' – a fundamental conflict between East and West.

After 9/11

In recent decades we have seen a similar anti-Muslim sentiment become acceptable in everyday life and institutions. This prejudice increased dramatically after the 9/11 attacks on the World Trade Center, New York, USA on 11 September, 2001. After the attacks, President George W. Bush of the USA evoked the spirit of the Crusades, saying, "this crusade, this war on terrorism, is going to take a while". His government went on to invade two Muslim-majority countries, Afghanistan and Iraq. Immediately Muslims around the world became stigmatised as dangerous terrorists as the world media and politicians echoed this sentiment time and time again.

The 9/11 Memorial at the site of the former World Trade Center complex pays tribute to those who died in the terrorist attacks of 11 September 2001, as well as the six people who were killed when the World Trade Center was bombed in February 1993.

As a result, today Islamophobia has become widespread in all areas of society. Islamophobia has even been described by some commentators as an 'industry', deliberately cultivated and institutionalised by those who wish to invade and exploit Muslim-majority lands. According to a June 2016 report released by the Council on American-Islamic Relations (CAIR) and the University of California Berkeley's Center for Race and Gender, more than **US$200 million** was pumped into the anti-Muslim propaganda industry between 2008 and 2013. That money, the report said, funded the activities of several dozen groups whose primary purpose is to "promote prejudice against, or hatred of, Islam and Muslims".

WHO IS AFFECTED BY
ISLAMOPHOBIA?

The effects of Islamophobia are far-reaching, with social, economic and political consequences for most Muslim-minority populations, as well as for people mistaken for Muslims. Men, women and children experience a very real fear and threat to their safety and position in society because of harmful and inaccurate stereotypes and prejudices about them and their religion.

Hate crimes against Muslims have surged in recent years, potentially damaging their physical and mental well-being. In addition, studies have shown that prejudice against Muslims can hold them back at school and in further education, and limit their success in the world of employment. It can even harm Muslim people's health as rules about sports kit can prevent, or deter, Muslim children from taking up sports where they are made to feel like outsiders because of what they wear.

Ibtihaj Muhammad, left, made history when she won team bronze in sabre fencing, the first Muslim-American to wear the hijab at the Olympics in 2016. Her parents encouraged her to take part in sports such as track and field and softball when she was growing up, but the fencing sports kit offered a solution to the problem of always looking different to others as it covers the body.

How does Islamophobia affect women?

Muslim women in particular bear the brunt of the effects of Islamophobia. They are routinely discriminated against in the workplace and are hence much more likely to be unemployed than women of other faiths, or no faith, with the same qualifications. Over half of the Islamophobic hate crimes that are reported are committed against women. Support groups also suggest that this figure could potentially be much higher since many incidents go unreported by victims.

There is also a mental toll to Islamophobia, with strong correlations being drawn between experiencing bigotry and having low confidence or anxiety. Many Muslims who are treated with contempt, fear or suspicion can begin to internalise feelings of low self-worth leading to broader long-term mental health issues. One Muslim woman we spoke to during our research for this book, who wanted to remain anonymous, described how fear of Islamophobic attacks had left her unable to leave the house and feeling like she was unwelcome in wider society. She felt that negative stereotypes of Muslims had damaged her confidence and made her fear for her physical safety.

Three young women having fun. But to some people, all they see are the headscarves, and that makes Muslim girls and women easy targets for Islamophobes.

WHAT IS STRUCTURAL ISLAMOPHOBIA?

Islamophobia can take many forms. When we think of Islamophobia, we may think of the family member who holds less-than-flattering views on Muslims or Islam, or the verbal abuse of a classmate. It is very important to think about how we can respond to and challenge individual incidents of Islamophobia like these. It is also important to remember that Islamophobia is structural, and that structural Islamophobia has a direct impact on the personal experiences of Muslims.

Structural Islamophobia refers to anti-Muslim racism and prejudice within a country's laws, institutions, a government's policies and in the media. For example, in France and Switzerland, laws ban the wearing of face veils or niqabs, even at a time when the wearing of face masks is mandatory in many places. In France the wearing of hijabs for girls under 18 and mothers on school trips is also banned. Structural or institutionalised hatred or suspicion of a group of people is very dangerous. It can lead to mass discrimination and, in extreme cases, to genocide or ethnic cleansing (the expulsion from an area or killing of members of an ethnic or religious group), as seen in the Central African Republic, where the UN described the ethnic cleansing of the Muslim population as 'a crime against humanity'.

TALKING POINTS

Take a look at these examples of Islamophobia around the world.
Have you heard of any of them?

Muslims in India

In 2019, the Indian government passed a law called the Citizen Amendment Act. The law is supposed to help refugees from the neighbouring Muslim-majority countries find a path to becoming Indian citizens. However, whilst the law is open to refugees from Sikh, Hindu and Christian faiths, among others, it excludes Muslim refugees, even those such as the Rohingya who are fleeing persecution.

In another move introduced by the Indian government in 2019, citizens in the Muslim-majority state of Assam were forced to provide paperwork proving their citizenship, which many poor people in the province simply do not have. This led to almost two million Muslims being made 'stateless', declared illegal foreigners in their own home and put in detention centres across the state.

Muslims in China

The Uyghurs are a Muslim-minority group living mostly in Xinjiang, north-west China. They have been oppressed for many years, but since the Iraq War (2003–2011), the Chinese government has stepped up its harassment of this minority group in what has been described as the worst modern-day human rights crisis. One in four of the population of 11 million Uyghurs has been forcibly detained in what the government calls 're-education camps' where they are forced to reject their religion, are tortured, have been sterilised or had organs removed in some cases, or been killed. Muslims are not allowed to fast or pray or name their sons 'Muhammad' and women are not allowed to wear the hijab.

Demonstrators gather in Hong Kong in December 2019 to show their support for Uyghur Muslims in China.

Muslims in the United States of America

In 2017 the then president, Donald Trump, introduced a Muslim ban, barring in-coming travellers from the Muslim-majority countries of Iran, Iraq, Libya, Somalia, Syria, Sudan and Yemen from entering the USA. The ban affected thousands of people, separating families and keeping people from their homes and loved ones.

In 2017, protestors at San Francisco International Airport in California, USA, demonstrated against President Trump's ban on travellers from several Muslim-majority countries entering the USA.

HOW DO ANTI-TERROR LAWS AFFECT MUSLIMS?

Many would argue that, in spite of national laws, Muslims are discriminated against on a political level in many countries. They say that governments have adopted the stance that Muslims and Islam are a threat that must be guarded against. As a result, new legislation has been put in place by several governments around the world that specifically targets Muslims.

Discrimination

Some members of the public suggest we need harsh laws in order to catch 'bad people' and so some governments respond to this pressure. What the general public don't see is the impact on the communities this legislation targets. For instance, since the year 2000, the Terrorism Act in the UK has targeted hundreds of thousands of Muslims based on what they look like and where they are travelling to. Turn to page 19 to read about the effects of the Muslim ban, introduced in the USA in 2017.

Can you imagine going on holiday, and being taken aside from the other passengers and treated as if you're a suspected criminal even though you have done nothing wrong?

For UK Muslims, it isn't just travelling that has become more difficult as a result of various terrorism laws. Some innocent Muslim families have had their citizenship taken away, been barred from returning to the UK, been barred from leaving the UK, been detained under a form of house arrest and had their bank accounts frozen or closed. Families have even been separated from their fathers who have been sent to live in other parts of the country. All these things can happen without a trial, by order of the Home Secretary, which then needs to be challenged in a so-called secret court that is closed to the public.

Prevent

Updated in 2011, the UK's Prevent programme has inspired many countries across the world to adopt similar policies in order to prevent radicalisation and terrorism. The idea is that if people are identified as potential threats before they commit a crime, the crime or act of terrorism can be prevented.

However, Prevent is one of the UK government's most controversial counter-terrorism initiatives, and the reality is that it often leads to Muslims being unjustly targetted, surveilled or treated with suspicion. The legislation requires public officials (teachers, nurses, doctors, etc) working in schools, universities, hospitals and local councils to report on individuals showing "radical tendencies".

This means that children and young people who express their beliefs are at risk of being reported to the authorities by their teachers, doctors and lecturers. Some children as young as three years old have been referred under the controversial programme.

TALKING POINTS

In 2019, a 13-year-old Muslim boy was questioned by UK school authorities about his affiliation with the extremist group Islamic State. It later emerged that he had been flagged up due to a statement he had made about 'eco-terrorism' during a class discussion.

• Can you imagine having to hide your beliefs or opinions? Or feeling too afraid to take part in a classroom discussion, in case you are reported as a potential terrorist?

• What effects do you think that might have on young Muslims growing up in a multicultural society?

WHAT ARE HATE CRIMES?

A hate crime is an act of hostility or violence directed at someone because of their disability, gender identity, race, sexual orientation, religion or any other perceived difference. There is no international definition but in 2019, the Organisation for Security and Cooperation in Europe (which works with 57 nations around the world) included these words in its report on hate crimes:

> Hate crimes are criminal acts motivated by bias or prejudice towards particular groups of people. To be considered a hate crime, the offence must meet two criteria: first, the act must constitute an offence under criminal law; second, the act must have been motivated by bias.

A hate crime could be:

- verbal abuse
- a physical attack
- incitement to hatred
- bullying and cyberbullying
- damage to property
- threatening behaviour.

Police forces advise the public to report ALL hate crimes, regardless of whether the victim sees the crime as a hate crime, or can present evidence.

9/11 revenge attacks

In the United States, the first revenge attack after 9/11 (see page 15) was not against a Muslim, but against Balbir Singh Sodhi, a Sikh-American. He was murdered at the petrol station he managed in Mesa, Arizona, USA. His killer said he wanted to "go out and shoot some towel heads".

This hate crime was one of many against Muslims, or people mistaken for Muslims, after 9/11. Sikh men, who grow long beards and wear turbans as a commitment to their faith, continue to be targets of hate crimes by those who mistake them for Muslims.

Religious buildings

Places of worship, community centres and faith schools can also be targets of hate crimes such as criminal damage, arson or by being defaced with offensive graffiti. In recent years, the remains of dead pigs have been left outside mosques on Fridays, the Muslim day of prayer, and during religious holidays, in order to cause offence to worshippers. Mosques have been broken into, had bomb threats, and, as we saw in New Zealand, many Muslim worshippers have sadly been killed in mosques.

Jewish synagogues continue to be the target of hate crimes against Jews by criminals who spray antisemitic graffiti, vandalise property or harm worshippers. In December 2019, there was a string of attacks on Jews and Jewish businesses.

"As a community, we regret the rise of hate speech in society ... Social media is polluted with xenophobia, Islamophobia, homophobia, misogyny, racism and antisemitism. Sadly, these things are connected.

This is a time for people of all backgrounds – of all faiths and of none – to stand united and show our determination that we do not tolerate prejudice, hate and division – on our streets or online."

Statement by the South Hampstead Synagogue, London, UK, after the attacks which took place in December 2019.

In March 2019, people gathered in Times Square, New York, USA, to protest against Islamophobia.

WHAT IS THE ROLE OF THE MEDIA?

Newspaper headlines, magazine articles, television programmes and social media all have a powerful effect on our ideas and opinions. Due to this power, it is important that the media be as fair and unbiased as possible, in order to allow us access to the facts so that we can make up our own minds.

The power of the media

Throughout history, the media has had the power to shape public opinion, to make a section of society look so bad that, eventually, hurting them, taking away their rights and even killing them is seen as an acceptable solution to national problems.

Does this remind you of anything you've read about so far in this book?

When a large percentage of the public gets all their knowledge from social media and other news outlets, it is very worrying that a large number of those news outlets constantly include small amounts of inaccurate knowledge of Islam in their so-called 'news reports'. They do it because they know it is an easy way to increase their readership, which in turn increases the wealth of the media outlets.

Inciting hatred

In April 2015, the British newspaper, *The Sun*, published an article in which Muslim migrants from war-torn Syria were referred to as "cockroaches" only hours before another migrant ship sank off the coast of Libya, killing some 800 people.

The article, along with thousands of other anti-foreigner articles published in British newspapers over the last 20 years, was condemned by the UN High Commissioner for Human Rights, Zeid Ra'ad Al Hussein, as an incitement to hatred.

A family of Syrian refugees fleeing civil war reaches the safety of the Greek island, Lesbos, after a traumatic sea crossing in a cramped dinghy.

Clear bias

It has long been noted that when a Muslim male commits a crime, such as a terrorist attack, his religious identity is highlighted in press reports and the Muslim community is called to account for its failure to 'root out' extremism.

However, when a similar crime is committed by a non-Muslim white male, there is no mention of his religion and his community is not asked to answer for him. In fact, the media often paints a sympathetic picture of the perpetrator as a mentally unstable, scarred or otherwise 'damaged' individual.

When you read something negative about Muslims, whether it is in a newspaper or on social media, don't believe it without investigating it yourself to check if it's actually true. When you see media that is unfairly treating Muslims or promoting anti-Muslim hate, make your voice heard by calling out the falsehood and making a complaint to the social media organisation, broadcaster or newspaper.

A study by the University of Alabama in the USA found that crimes committed by Muslim extremists receive 375 per cent more media attention than those committed by others.

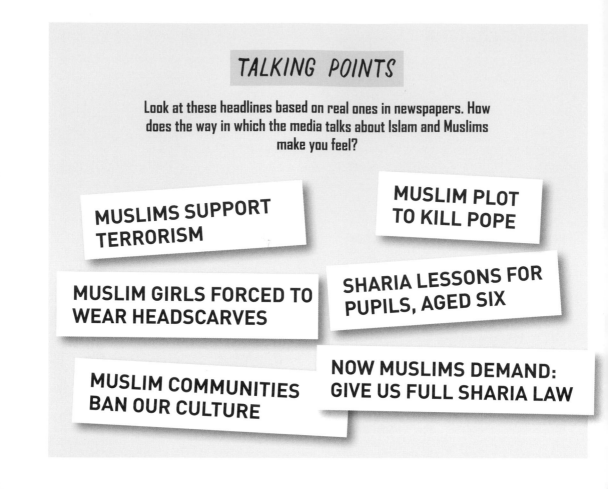

What is Sharia?

In two of the headlines above there's a reference to Sharia and Sharia law. Let's look at what Sharia is and why some newspapers present it as a threat.

The literal meaning of Sharia is 'the path to be followed' and those who follow it see it as an essential guide for living according to God's wishes.

Sharia is derived from the Qur'an, the holy book of Islam, the teachings and sayings of the prophet Muhammad (pbuh) and the rulings of Islamic scholars.

It is divided into sections to act as a guide to every aspect of a Muslim person's life, from acts of worship to how to behave as a business person, from marriage and divorce to food, drink and the punishment of crimes.

Why is Sharia seen as a threat?

Throughout history, people and communities have been taught to fear 'others' or those who are perceived to differ from them. As we'll see, Islamophobia has been able to flourish in our society by the media playing on those fears. For example, hashtags such as 'Creeping Sharia' on social media, absurdly serve to claim that Muslims or Sharia are taking over or attacking the way of life of a non-Muslim-majority country. Such claims are used to vilify immigrant communities and make people believe that society is changing for the worse. There is no move by Muslims living across the world to make Sharia law universal.

Unfortunately, incorrect assumptions still make people anxious and can lead to headlines such as those opposite. That's why it's important to think about the assumptions we might be making about others and have discussions with each other in a way that rejects fear – or phobia – of people who are different from us, and which start from a point of mutual respect.

Debunking myths

Take two other common myths about Islam and Muslims reflected in the headlines on page 26

1) The myth that Muslims support terrorism and that Islam promotes violence:

WRONG: Islam views murder as a crime and one of the worst sins against Allah (God).

2) The myth that Muslim girls are forced to wear headscarves:

WRONG: most girls and women are free to choose to wear the hijab, although in Iran women have to wear the hijab by law, and in some countries, such as France, it is illegal for girls under 18 to wear it.

Research by Lancaster University in the UK found that, for every positive or neutral mention of Islam or Muslims in the British press, there are 21 negative references.

TALKING POINTS

Have you ever formed an opinion based on something you've heard or seen in the media?

How do you think reporters can avoid Islamophobia and other forms of stereotyping and bias in their reporting?

HOW DO WE CHALLENGE DISCRIMINATION AND PREJUDICE?

Remember the two levels of Islamophobia we explored earlier, the individual and the structural (see page 18)? Sometimes, it can feel like there is little we can do to challenge these types of discrimination; so much of what is happening is out of our control and seems to be going on behind the scenes. But there is a way that every one of us can challenge discrimination and prejudice and work towards peace and justice for all.

On a personal level

Every one of us has control over our own actions – sometimes that is the only thing we do have control over, especially as children and young people. So we all have the power to think, to reflect, to form our own opinions, to act in a way that is in line with our conscience and our values.

Every one of us interacts with the media on a regular basis – but we can choose which media to give our attention to.

- We can call out examples of Islamophobia and prejudice in the media and within our communities.

- We can recognise racism and discrimination and call it out.

- We can refuse to participate in racist or Islamophobic jokes or banter.

- We can address our own prejudices and open our minds to other viewpoints so that we can learn more about the values, views and opinions of others. That way, we pave the way for a more egalitarian, diverse society, one in which we all feel safe.

"No one is born hating another person because of the colour of his skin, or his background, or his religion. People must learn to hate, and if they can learn to hate, they can be taught to love, for love comes more naturally to the human heart than its opposite."

Nelson Mandela, South Africa's
first black president

On a political level

The political system is meant to represent us and ensure the kind of society we all want to live in: one in which we all feel safe. That means that power structures should be held to account and unfair policies should be questioned and debated. Political parties must make sure that people with racist and Islamophobic views are not allowed to become members of political parties or stand for election as political representatives at any level of local or national politics.

You may feel like this is out of your control now, but you will be able to vote in elections in a few years' time. You can also engage with politics by writing to your MP to protest against political injustices. It is important that you are aware of issues such as racism, intolerance and Islamophobia, so that you can get a clearer idea of the kind of society you want to build and be a part of.

TALKING POINTS

As a young person, you have the power to prevent negative stereotypes from affecting the way you relate to individuals and communities.

You have the power to educate yourself and others.

You have the power to do things differently, to create a better future for all.

You have the power to choose hope over hate.

GLOSSARY

anti-semitism discrimination or prejudice against Jews

Aryan in the context of Nazi Germany this term was used to refer to non-Jewish caucasians

bias prejudice for or against an individual or group

burka a garment covering the whole body worn by some Muslim women

colonisation the act of taking over an area and taking control of the people living there

conscience someone's sense of what is right and wrong

discrimination the prejudicial treatment of an individual or group

extremist describes an individual or group holding extreme views or advocating taking extreme action

fatwa a legal pronouncement in Islam, made by someone with the authority to do so

genocide the organised killing of a group of people

heretic a person who holds opinions that go against traditional religious doctrines

hijab a head covering worn by some Muslim women

Holy Land the land, including Jerusalem, located in modern-day Israel, Palestine and Jordan, that is sacred to Christians, Jews and Muslims

human rights rights that belong to each individual person

intolerance refusal to accept the beliefs and views of other people that differ from your own

Latin mass a Roman Catholic religious service celebrated in Latin

legislation laws

nationalism devotion to your nation

niqab a face covering worn by some Muslim women

Ottoman Empire the empire that ruled a large part of Eastern Europe and the Middle East between 1299 and 1923

pacifism opposition to war or violence

pilgrimage a journey to a place of religious significance.

Pope the head of the Roman Catholic Church

propaganda biased information used to promote a particular political stance

Protestant (religion) a follower of a form of Christianity that separated from the Roman Catholic Church

Qur'an the holy book of Islam, written in Arabic. It contains the word of Allah as revealed to the Prophet Muhammad (pbuh)

Ramadan Muslim holy month of fasting

Roman Catholic follower of the form of Christianity that has the pope as its head

Sharia Islamic law

stereotype an oversimplified idea of someone or something

traitor someone who has committed treason, the crime of betraying their country

Further information

REPORTING ISLAMOPHOBIA

Islamophobia is a hate crime and should be reported to the **police**. There are also a number or organisations such as Mend UK or Hope Not Hate (see website addresses below) that you can contact; they will log the incident and offer any emotional or practical support.

Childline has started creating a safe space offering help for children who may be experiencing discrimination or hate as a result of their religion or appearance. The helpline number is 0800 1111. The website address is below.

Ofcom's job is to make sure that the press is accurate, unbiased and impartial. You can make a complaint to Ofcom if you feel that a piece of journalism is biased or discriminatory.

Sometimes victims of crimes do not want to report what's happened as they do not wish to go over the painful experience or may be fearful of speaking out. In such incidents it is best to respect people's wishes and think of other ways you can offer support to them.

BOOKS

What is Race? Who Are Racists? Why Does Skin Colour Matter? And Other Big Questions by Claire Heuchan and Nikesh Shukla (Wayland, 2020)

Amazing Muslims Who Changed the World by Burhana Islam (Puffin, 2020)

WEBSITES

www.ourmigrationstory.org.uk
Website presenting the stories of generations of migrants who came to, and shaped, the British Isles.

Mend UK (Muslim Engagement and Development)
mend.org.uk

Hope Not Hate
hopenothate.org.uk

Childline
childline.org.uk

oic-oci.org
The Organization of Islamic Cooperation (OIC) describes itself as 'the Collective Voice of the Muslim World' and is made up of 57 member states. The OIC declared 15th March (the anniversary of the Christchurch mosque attacks) to be the International Day to Combat Islamophobia.

INDEX